Sh... ...ezy

Eeek

bly

Bdd

Bdd

Ghostly

Breathless

Puff

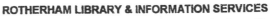

Thanks for helping the Baa'd
Petra, Lina and Joe, Rachel and Mercedes

BAA FOR BEGINNERS
A HUTCHINSON BOOK 0 09 176909 4

Published in Great Britain by Hutchinson,
an imprint of Random House Children's Books

This edition published 2005

1 3 5 7 9 10 8 6 4 2

RANDOM HOUSE CHILDREN'S BOOKS
61–63 Uxbridge Road, London W5 5SA
A division of The Random House Group Ltd

RANDOM HOUSE AUSTRALIA (PTY) LTD
20 Alfred Street, Milsons Point, Sydney,
New South Wales 2061, Australia

RANDOM HOUSE NEW ZEALAND LTD
18 Poland Road, Glenfield, Auckland 10, New Zealand

RANDOM HOUSE (PTY) LTD
Endulini, 5A Jubilee Road, Parktown 2193, South Africa

THE RANDOM HOUSE GROUP Limited Reg. No. 954009
www.kidsatrandomhouse.co.uk

A CIP catalogue record for this book is available from the British Library.

Printed in Singapore

Baa
for
Beginners

Deborah Fajerman

HUTCHINSON

London Sydney Auckland Johannesburg

The language of sheep is called Baa and every single word is baa.

There are many different ways to speak Baa.

But when sheep are lambs
they only know one kind.

So their teacher Mrs Ramsbottom
takes them on a field trip.

When Baa is near
it's loud and clear.

When Baa is far
it's hard to hear.

When a lamb is all alone,
its baa sounds small and thin . . .

But Baa sounds big
and fat when all the
lambs join in!

Baa is shivery
when it snows . . .

and is whisked right away when the wind blows.

When sheep are climbing
they don't have enough
breath to baaaa . . .

They just huff and puff
and puff and huff.

Baa goes rather wobbly when it's dark as night.

But Baa is calm and flat
when the sun is bright.

When sheep sit on the grass
their bottoms go bright green.

A bubble bath with bubbly baas
makes their bottoms clean.

Mrs Ramsbottom has
finished the field trip.
It is time for the lambs
to take their Baa exam.

They all get a gold star.
And now it's time for their very best baas . . .

The ones they say to their ma's and pa's!

Near

Far

Thin

Fat

Wobbly

Calm